Emily De Ford

OF THRONE AND FOOT-STOOL

The Bible tells us that Heaven is God's Throne and the Earth is His Foot-Stool. The poems in this booklet vary in content from the ridiculous to the sublime - from earthly happenings to Heavenly aspirations.

We earthlings would do well to be mindful of Heaven, remembering that the temporal is decision ground for the Eternal. It is my hope that your sojourn on God's Foot-Stool will be pleasant and profitable, and that by the grace of our Lord Jesus Christ, we will meet at His Throne.

"...I looked, and behold, a door was opened in Heaven, and the voice...said, 'Come up here'..."

Revelation 4:1

Mrs. Don Mathis
Box 44A Route 7
Burwell, Nebraska 68823

© Copyright 1972

MEN OF LIKE PASSIONS

I used to think (before God's word I'd read)
That the men of the Bible (who've gone on ahead)
Were perfect and faultless - their lives pure and true -
That they were different from me and from you.
But when I had studied and found out the truth,
I found they weren't perfect - neither old man nor youth.
They were men of like passions, just such as we -
Those folks in the Bible were human, like me!

Men of like passions - does it come as a shock
That Moses got mad and pounded the rock;
That Abraham to his wife was not fair,
And Nehemiah in anger, pulled people's hair!?
Too, there was Peter, who bragged and who lied.
Then, stricken with shame, he bitterly cried.
There was David, who stole another man's wife
And lived to regret it the rest of his life.

Even the Apostle, our hero named Paul
Knew what it was like to stumble and fall.
He had to say 'sorry' for calling a name.
(Tho' the men who bugged him were more to blame.)
But time would fail me to mention them all,
For each man in the Bible had his own fall.
Tho' God tells of their good, He hides not their shame,
To teach us today that all flesh is the same.

> Only One - the Spotless Son of God
> Was sinless, as this earth He trod.

But all the rest - in the past or today
Were men of like passions - with feet made of clay -
The statesman, the labor'r, the preacher, the bum -
Each man to the foot of the Cross must come.
And, there, by the blood of His Infinite Son,
God cleanses each one and a new life's begun.
Then in Heaven we'll sing with Abram and Paul,
"Twas only by grace that we got here at all!"

THE QUICKENING

Well do I remember
When I was great with child,
The throb of life within –
Beating strong, tapping mild;
A silent, sweet reminder
That I had given room,
And life beside my own
Was pulsing in my womb.

From union with the one
Who's love was strong and true,
The seed had taken root,
And life within now grew.
No doubt could now remain
When that inner throb was felt –
New life was surely there –
My future clearly spelt.

Today, this brings to mind
(Tho' no baby's coming on),
A truth that God reveals
In His Word about His Son.
There's One Who lives within
All folks who grant Him room –
A vibrant, pulsing Life,
Sure's a babe within a womb.

United with the Father,
His Word the wondrous Seed –
The womb of faith now pulsates
With His own Life indeed.
No doubt for one who knows
This Vital Force within –
This is Life Eternal,
This Quick'ning shall not end.

TREAD LIGHTLY

Tread lightly, child,
The ice ahead is thin,
And only one unguarded step
Could plunge you deep within.

Speak gently, child,
With words of cautious tone.
Today's humiliation,
Tomorrow could be your own.

Grasp loosely, child,
The precious toys of earth.
That thing you prize so highly
Could so quickly lose it's worth.

Think rightly, child,
Of friendships you count rare.
Even closest earthly ties
Could become to you a snare.

Walk wisely, child,
Nor be at ease in Zion.
For tomorrow you could face
The Devil's roaring lion.

Hold tightly, child,
And cling in helpless trust
To the blessed hand of Jesus,
The wise One and the Just.

Trust fully, child,
He's been this way before.
Uncertain tho' the path appears,
It leads to Heaven's shore.

A WORD TO THE WIVES

If you, like me, are a preacher's wife
(A blessed privilege - a busy life) -
A part of your duty, you will find,
Is to speak these words from time to time -
When hubby's depressed, ready to screech,
"My dear, you must practice what you preach."

When folks don't listen nor change their life,
'Tis then that the preacher needs a wife
To prod him along, lest faith grows small,
"Keep on, dear, don't throw in the towel -
It will take a while, their hearts to reach,
Mean time, you must practice what you preach."

He's preached on joy and he's preached on trust.
He's preached on faith for all of the just.
But his smile of joy has all but fled
And worry now lines his brow instead.
It is then we wives must still beseech,
"Take heart and practice what you preach."

Words fitly spoke - like apples of gold,
Spoken before a warm heart grows cold,
Spoken when lures of this earth creep near,
Spoken to him when none else can hear.
"Dear you're beyond the enemy's reach -
Stand firm and practice what you preach."

Brag on his sermons, nor dwell on faults.
Pray for him much when Satan assaults.
Speak of mistakes in tones hushed and sweet.
Tell him you're glad to be his help-meet.
Be faith-ful, kind, as God word teaches,
Help him to practice what he preaches.

THE HEART OF A STRANGER
Exodus 23:9

Have you ever been in a crowded place
And searched in vain for an old friend's face?
Have you ever felt alone in a crowd,
Tho' the talk was pleasant, the laughter loud,
Tho' people were kind and included you,
But you longed for a friend whom you really knew?
A familiar voice and a sparkling smile,
Someone with whom you could chat awhile,
And talk of good times you'd shared in the past –
Memories that new friends never could grasp?

Have you wondered just when you'd feel at peace,
The ache for familiar surroundings cease?
And then, when you tho't you'd conquered your fears
A haunting mem'ry would bring back the tears?
Friend, it takes time to feel right at home
When you've pulled up stakes and been made to roam.
And really, now, it just wouldn't be fair
To forget the past with never a care.
Your life has been molded, formed by each friend
That you left behind; This strangeness will end
And you'll be richer in friendships, for sure,
With the new that inspire, the old that endure.

THE NEST

Lord, must you stir this lovely nest?
I'm so content - please let me rest.
My roots are deep - I'm satisfied,
Loathe to be stirred, or sorely tried.
Don't rouse me now - just let me be.
I'll still pay tithes and pray to Thee.

> "..As an eagle stirreth
> up her nest, fluttereth
> over her young, spread-
> eth abroad her wings,
> taketh them, beareth
> them on her wings...."

But Lord, I fear to leave this nest!
How can a change be for the best?
Why does the nest feel strange, un-real?
What is this restlessness I feel?
Is this Thy voice that calls to me,
That bids me rise and follow Thee?

> "..The Lord alone did lead them
> ...He made them ride on the
> high places....."

Oh, Lord! - Your wings <u>are</u> bearing me! -
And far below, the nest <u>I</u> see!
(Strange that I should fear Thy leading,
Close my ears to patient pleading.)
For here I am - who needs a nest?
Soaring, rejoicing - Thy will <u>is</u> best!

HOUSES OR HEARTS??

What do you see when you look at a town?
When you're seeking a place to settle down?
Do you look for fine homes and stores well stocked?
For grassy front yards and shady green blocks?
Do you seek the heights in music and arts,
Seeing the houses, forgetting the hearts?

A town is made out of flesh, and not bricks -
It's made from people, not stones and not sticks.
For within a very humble dwelling,
There may be the sweetest music swelling;
Perhaps not perfect in note or in parts,
But that which springs from contented hearts.

Behind a machine, a desk or a drill,
Under a grease-rack, beside a mill,
Back of a counter, a broom or a wheel
There's one who cares how another may feel.
For a town's not made of houses and marts.
It's made from people - It's made out of hearts.

When judging a town, be it large or small,
What's seen on the surface is not the all;
For like a friendship that's lasted for years -
A town is mellowed by its' joys and tears.
So judge it with care before you depart -
Don't look at the houses - look at the hearts.

EMMANUEL – GOD WITH US

When the last Christmas Carol's resounded,
    And the manger scene's all packed away,
When the tinsel is swept off the carpet,
    And the tree is dragged out to stay;

When the excitement of Christmas is over,
    And the mundane of life sets the tone,
Praise the Lord, our wonderful Saviour,
    Our Emmanuel is still with His own!

NATIVITY SCENE

While angels pull their knee-sox high,
Toothless shepherds watch nearby.
Mary, Joseph, ill at ease,
Bathrobed wisemen on their knees.
Cotton-draped and wiggly sheep,
Nervous teachers, vigil keep.
Other angels, soon will come,
Weary-winged and chewing gum.
Chubby inn-man slams the door
As age-old story's told once more.

Thoughtful watchers see beyond
Manger scene, traditions fond,
And see the Life, the Truth, the Way
Who grants us Christmas every day.

THAT VITAL RECITAL

Nervous children
Sweaty palms
Clucking teacher
Beaming Moms
Doting Grandmas
Patient Dads
Restless babies
Toothless lads
First-time nylons
Skimpy skirts
Plastered cow-licks
Sunday shirts
Jigs and polkas
Minuets
Clap politely
More duets
Trills and dirges
Lagging clock
Thumps and fumbles
Aching Bach
Notes remembered
Notes forgot
Some have got it
Some have not.

SPIT BATHS

Of all the curses known to youth
(I tell you this in somber truth)
There's none that ever could be worse
Than having Mom reach in her purse,
Take out her hanky, start her search,
And give us spit-baths on the way to church.

At home our Dad has guaranteed
That all us boys are clean, indeed.
He's checked us all with manly skill,
And we're all satisfied - until
Our Mom begins her sputt-ring search
And we get spit-baths on the way to church!

Oh, would some pow'r us deliver
When Dad starts up the fam'ly flivver,
And we're all dressed in Sunday best
And Mom begins her weekly quest,
Attacking while we yelp and lurch,
Bestowing spit-baths on the way to church!

I'll have you know, when I'm a Dad
And all my boys are Sunday-clad,
E'en tho' they're smeared with jam or hash
And have a milky-way mustache,
I'll make my wife just keep her perch -
There'll be no spit-baths on the way to church!

THAT'S MY BOY

THAT'S MY BOY - the husky one in the nurse's arms -
The cute red faced one who's squalling out new-born alarms.
THAT'S MY BOY - that wiggly one on the little red chair,
The one who's peeking thru' his fingers during prayer.
THAT'S MY BOY - with the dirty face and grass-stained pants,
The one who caught the ball - in my geranium plants.
THAT'S MY BOY - the one who keeps marching out of step,
Who's tooting way off key, full of mischievous pep.
THAT'S MY BOY - up there, with pride shining in his eyes -
The one who's being given the champion's prize.
THAT'S MY BOY - I'm sorry, it won't happen again.
I promise, sir, that I shall have a talk with him.
THAT'S MY BOY - the muddy fellow there on the ground,
The one who made that last spectacular touch-down!
THAT'S MY BOY - Say, did you just hear that jet roar?
He's doing all he can to end this awful war.
THAT'S MY BOY - and the girl he chose to be his bride,
And that's my little grand son, right by his Daddy's side.
THAT'S MY BOY - with all those medals on his chest,
There because he never feared to do his very best.
THAT'S MY BOY - he's to be the honored one today.
All too quickly have boy-hood seasons fled away.
THAT'S MY BOY - he's been asked to sit there on the stage.
My, his hair is gray - he's begun to show my age!
THAT'S MY BOY - and to think that he is mine!
I'm so very proud to have raised a son so fine.
THAT'S MY BOY - Oh!, they're bowing now for prayer -
And that's my little grand son who just fell off his chair!

SECOND GRADERS

Chipmunk teeth
Freckled snoots
Skinned-up knees
Muddy boots.

Gnawed-on pens
Tousled locks
Grubby hands
Rumpled sox.

Modern Math
Finger-smeared
Doctor Seuss
Doggy-eared.

Teachers sigh,
"Try-again."
Pupils frown,
"Is it ten?"

Thirty-five
Wiggle-warts
Make hours long
Tempers short.

DISTANCE LENDS ENCHANTMENT

"There was just an orange in my sock,"
My Dad repeats again,
"And thankful you should be, young man,
You didn't live back then."

"Our Christmas days were lean", he says,
"Slim pickin's was the rule."
And long and lonely were the miles
My Father trudged to school.

Drifts were higher, sun was hotter,
And longer were the days.
Foes were mightier, Soldiers braver,
Bloodier were the frays.

Work was harder, wages smaller,
But folks were more content.
Why kids were tickled pink to share
A stick of peppermint.

My Dad is sure that bye gone days
Gave forth a brighter hue.
I wonder, tho', could distance
Lend enchantment to the view?

THREE GUESSES

The fam'ly says the meal's delicious
'Twas cooked to suit their fondest wishes,
They're each so full they're stomach squishes,
But who's left to do the dinner dishes?

    (Three guesses!)

Dad's got to trim that old spirea.
Bill's got a test about Crimea.
Sis suddenly gets the diarrhea.
Who's left when all have said, "I'll see ya!"?

    (Three guesses!)

BUT....
Who says that she has had enough?
Who bellers with a voice that's gruff?
Who nabs each one and calls their bluff?
Who meekly comes to do their stuff?

    (Three guesses!)

ASPIRATION - PERSPIRATION

"This mowing lawn is sissy stuff -
It's for the dudes - I've had enuff!
As soon as I can get a chance,
I'll get a job out on a ranch! -
A job where horse and man are tuff
Where sweat smells strong and work is rough!"

Reminded of my days of yore,
When life at home, was too, a bore,
I held my peace 'til came the day
My would-be-cow-boy went his way.
He sallied forth as to the war,
And left me leaning on the mower.

One day I stopped where son had gone,
To see how he was getting on,
I found him toiling like a man,
And sweating as the male sex can;
He'd tuffed it out since early dawn,
For the ranch, it has a good sized lawn.

FIVE BOYS

Over at last.
The long days past.
Gone awkward gait
And tedious wait,
Shapeless dresses,
Excited guesses.
The battle's won –
We've one more son.
No hoped-for curls.
(But who likes girls?!)
Bring out the blue.
(Hate pink, don't you?!)
Prepare for noise,
We've got five boys!

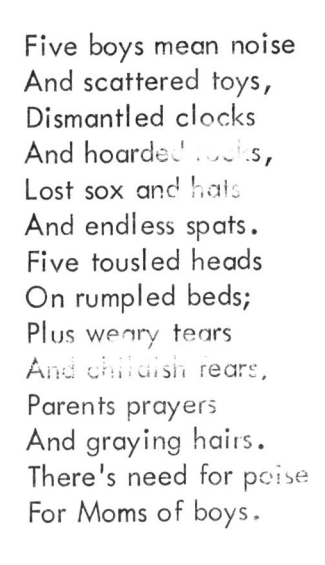

Five boys mean noise
And scattered toys,
Dismantled clocks
And hoarded rocks,
Lost sox and hats
And endless spats.
Five tousled heads
On rumpled beds;
Plus weary tears
And childish rears,
Parents prayers
And graying hairs.
There's need for poise
For Moms of boys.

Five boys mean joys
Despite the noise,
The hectic din
And impish grin.
For fam'ly fun,
Games lost, games won,
A private chat,
A homeless cat,
A new-found friend,
A toy to mend,
A tear to dry,
A grateful sigh,
Bring priceless joys
To Moms of boys.

THOSE BOYS

THOSE BOYS! I mutter from under their bed,
As I rake out a dust-ball, hoping it's dead!

THOSE BOYS! I shriek at my floor, freshly mopped.
"Gee, Mom, the puppy's milk - it sorta slopped."

THOSE BOYS! I grumble from their closet door -
Freshly washed shirts all over the floor.

THOSE BOYS! I nag as I view muddy jeans
And dig from the washer, marbles and beans.

THOSE BOYS! I moan as they're all late for lunch,
Then bring in their pals, not one, but a bunch.

THOSE BOYS! I sigh as I ponder that lump
And under the sheet, a puppy tail thumps.

THOSE BOYS! I fume from a flooded bath floor,
While soap-suds gurgle from under the door.

THOSE BOYS! I say it year out, year in.
Will these years ever pass, and these boys be men?

THOSE BOYS! Oh, for the day when they'll be grown -
No bugs, no mud, no collections of stones.

NO BOYS! A nice neat house, quiet and still.
An empty table, where nothing gets spilled.

NO BOYS! But lonely feelings ev'ry day,
While list'ning for them to bound in from play.

NO BOYS! But three fine men, dear Lord, I ask.
Help me daily to succeed in this task.

NO BOYS! But men who'll bring me pride and joy,
Who'll make me glad I mothered "THOSE BOYS!"

HOW COME??

How come -
When I need an errand run,
No kids show up - not even one.
But when my lid is almost flipping,
And I feel my halo slipping,
There are kids around, galore,
Plus seven at the door,
But no helpers.

How come -
When my call comes in at last,
And I need a pencil fast,
A search thru' chair interiors
Yields pop-corn (quite inferior),
Plus combs and dolly dresses,
But deep in those recesses,
Are no pencils.

How come -
When sister's hair is tangled,
And the bell at school has jangled,
I may search upstairs and down,
But no comb will be around.
I'll find stuff I needed once before,
Pencils, ball-point-pens, galore,
But not a comb.

How come -
My game's a loss, without a win -
A life-long search for odds and ends.
When I find the end, I've lost the odd,
It's good my head's screwed to my bod.
This life of mine is slightly garbled -
When I find my buttons, I've lost my marbles!

NO BOYS -- NO FUN

The tho't, it comes to me,
How simple life would be,
How neat, how free from noise,
If there were no little boys.

No sun-burned, tooth-less guys
With mischief in their eyes,
In wrong-side-out T-shirts,
To track in dust and dirt.

No need for Mom to fume,
At cluttered, junk-strewn room;
No sox in crazy places,
Shoes with frazzled laces.

No dirty under-wear
Beneath the comp'ny chair,
No frenzied school-book search,
No un-zipped pants in church.

No pets, no bugs, no pups,
No busted china cups.
No deafn'ing shout, "We won!",
No noise, no boys, no fun!

DON'T LIBERATE ME!

Don't liberate me from my feminine chains
Nor make me compete with masculine brains.
Don't make me join those wild women in sweaters –
I want to stay home and polish my fetters.

Don't say, "Come, be independent, be bolder"! –
I enjoy a good cry on my hubby's shoulder.
Don't liberate me from my ironing and sink –
That's the best place in the world for me to think.

Don't sign me up to campaign in some booth –
I might miss the thrill of a baby's first tooth.
Don't send me out to demand equal rights –
Junior might need me to help fix his kites.

I don't have time to discuss women's lib –
I must finish this quilt for my grand-child's crib.
Don't liberate me from my husband's arms –
Or from baking a pie, or a school-boy's charms.

Don't deny me the fun of family fests –
Nor the bitter-sweet thrill when kids leave the nest.
Don't liberate me – I love my fetters.
God made me a help-meet – there's nothing better!

OF ALL THINGS!!

Of all things!
      A tiny black kitten afloat in the suds –
      Hissing and swirling among all the duds.
      (She'd gone to sleep on a pile of towels,
      So Mom fished her out and soothed her howls.)

Of all things!
      A 10-gallon hat a-soak in the sink!
      (It's too big, Mom, and it needs to shrink.)
      "But it's a brand-new hat!", aghast Mom said.
      "Yup!" – and the dripping hat is plunked on his
                                           head.

Of all things!
      The cruddiest old pair of men's work shoes
      Worn by a girl who would flatly refuse
      To wear something neat that Mom would approve.
      ('Cause Mom's ideas just aren't in the groove.)

Of all things!
      Chocolate cake for a mangy old dog
      Smelly white mice, and a slimy pet frog.
      Dirty ears after an hour in the tub.
      Elaborate plans for a 'Boy-Haters' Club.

Of all things!
      A pup in the bed – a snake in a box!
      Father at church in mis-mated sox!
      Sis's new brush for the horse's mane;
      Mom's very best bowl to feed him his grain.

Of all things!
      Mom's learned thru' the years to take in stride,
      The odd-ball things that shock feminine pride.
      For with seven kids on her apron strings,
      She's found, life gaily consists of 'all things'.

LOOKING FOR THE PREACHER?

You ask me where the preacher lives? –
The one with all the kids?
His house is where those marching boys
Are banging kettle lids.

It's there, where all those bikes are dropped
On top the struggling grass,
And that lanky kid with freckles
Is running for a pass....

Where that line of patched-up blue-jeans
Is flapping in the breeze;
And those kids a-playing Tarzan
Are scrambling up the trees;

Where that greasey bunch of ten year olds
Try their new go-cart,
And that tear-streaked toddler on the steps
Is wailing out his heart;

Where that giggly group of teen-aged girls
Fill the old porch swing,
Watching for a certain boy,
Hoping for the phone to ring.

You're looking for the preacher's house?
Stranger, you can't fail –
Follow the noise down yonder street,
Watch for a kid-strewn trail;

Stop at the house with the barking dog,
And call out clear and loud.
(The preacher's the one with greying hair –
The tallest of the crowd.)

THE LOSER WHO WINS

When you haven't won at all
And you're disappointed, so –
And you've had to take a fall
Right in front of folks you know.....

When you cannot blame a soul,
And you feel so low-down, cheap –
When you've failed to reach your goal,
And you're underneath the heap;

You still come up a-winnin'
Even tho' you've come in last,
If you'll take your loss a-grinnin'
And don't grumble 'bout what's past.

For you can be a hero
In your children's trusting eyes
Tho' you have drawn a zero
And have failed to get a prize.

For a man is not a champ
Just by trophies on his shelf;
He can be a low-down scamp
If he loses to himself.

It's how he takes his losses,
How he acts thru' thick and thin,
It's how he bears his crosses,
That determines if he'll win.

And your kids, your friends, your wife
Will forget you didn't win
All the races of this life,
If you'll wear the victor's grin!

MY GLORY-CROWN

"Boy, Mom, you sure are getting gray."
My grown-up kids are wont to say.
I can't deny their candid view,
But change that gray, I shall not do.

Gray hairs my Lord does not disdain,
For in His word, He makes it plain
That hoary hair's a glory crown
So I'll not tint it back to brown.

Each hair of white I've fairly won -
'Tis nothing some beautician's done!
The stress and strain of mother-hood,
The battles fought, the foes with-stood;

The mid-night cries for loving care,
The child-hood woes to heal and share,
The teen-age ardor freely spent,
Fools-hill that can't be circumvent -

All these have turned my hair to gray.
I'd have it not another way.
My hair of gray shall not be spurned;
For it's a "birth"-right that I've earned.

IT'S GREAT TO BE IN LOVE

Oh, it's great to be in love,
When you're young and full of pep,
When your skies are clear above,
And you walk with bouyant step;
When you feel you've got it made
And your world is bright and green,
When one's a gay young blade
And the other's just a teen.

It's great to hear 'your song',
And meander, holding hands,
So sure that nothing wrong
Could dim your future plans.
When your wedding rings still gleam
And life looks bright and gay,
When you share your fondest dreams
And laughter greets each day.

But it's great to be in love
When the years have left their mark;
And your hair is thin above
And you've sorta lost your spark;
When your bank account is drained
And your arms are full of babies,
When your confidence has waned,
Your 'yesses' turned to 'maybes'.

It's great to get a thrill
When you hear that step again,
To feel your heart stand still
As you trade a knowing grin.
It's great to get a hug
Tho' your out of shape and lumpy,
To feel secure and snug
Tho' fashion says you're dumpy;

                        Cont'd.

When your wedding ring's worn thru
And your hands are gnarled and rough,
When your dreams have not come true,
And walking makes you puff.
It's great to have a song,
Tho' your own is out of style,
It's great to tag along
And enjoy each other's smile.

It's great to be in love,
In spite of trials and tears,
To fit like hand in glove,
To be mellowed by the years.
It's great to be in love,
With your hearts so firmly set,
That when beckoned up above,
You part with no regret.

KITCHEN ALTAR

I've an altar in my kitchen –
A place for me alone
To worship ev'ry busy day,
And make my heart-needs known.

It's there my foes are faced & fought
It's there my battles' won.
It's there my tears are often shed
For daughter or for son.

There at my kitchen altar,
(It's made of stainless steel),
My Father hears me when I pray,
Tho' I never bow nor kneel.

I'm glad I have this altar –
A place to thank and think;
For my most effective praying
Is at my kitchen sink.

LORD, DON'T ANSWER

Lord, answer not all prayers I say
For I know not oft how to pray,
And I might plead some earthly goal
That would bring leanness to my soul.

So guide me as I make my prayers.
May they be free from earthly cares
And temporal wants that can be seen –
I fear to have a soul grown lean.

A soul, well-fed, please grant to me
E'en tho' you may deny some plea.
I'm short of sight, and tears may roll,
But don't send leanness to my soul.

(...He gave them their request, but
sent leanness into their soul.
Psalm 106:15)

ALREADY??

My daughter? Home-coming queen?
My daughter? - A favorite Teen?

That squalling bit of humanity
Who's formula was never right?
Who sucked her thumb for security
And clutched a blanket day and night?

That spindly-legged little tease?
That chatter-box with mischeivous eyes?
With straggly-hair and skinned up knees,
Who played with dolls and hated guys?

My daughter? Wearing the crown?
Dear Lord, where have the years all gone?

ONE WHOM THE LORD LOVES

I saw him standing there alone
Beside the body of his soldier son –
A humble man, respected sage,
Tall and straight despite his age.

A man who'd gone thru' chastening sore,
For death had come his way before,
Had left him widowed, children small –
He knew the taste of worm-wood, gall.

And now to lay aside his boy –
A lad so young – a fleeting joy.
I watched and wondered if this man
Would see this, too, as God's good plan;

Or, in resentment, would he shout,
"This is too much!" – God's comfort flout?
But no, I saw him lift his head
And heard no curse, but praise instead.

I heard him quote the ageless word,
Learned in past from Sovereign Lord,
"My way is best, in spite of rod –
Be still and know that I am God!"

MOM'S HANDS

My Mom has aged so gracefully –
She's slim, attractive, chic.
Her hair is streaked with gray,
But her laugh is young and quick.

Yes, Mom is well preserved,
Despite all time's demands,
But her history is told
When you're looking at her hands.

For tho' my Mom could pass
For a woman used to ease,
Yet her hands reveal a tale
That not every person sees.

Those hands have fed and milked
A stubborn Jersey cow,
Have soothed a feverish child
With a measle-spotted brow.

They've steered a Farmall tractor,
A blind old horse, a truck,
Diapered 5 babies,
And pushed the car when it got stuck.

They've mowed away hay
In the peak of the barn
And stashed away sox –
Too busy to darn.

They've made over dresses
From oddest assortment
And swatted kids pants
When teaching deportment;

Cleaned up messes
From kids and their pets,
Wrote out the checks
To pay up the debts;
    Cont'd.

Popped bushels of corn
For Sunday night snacks,
Papered the walls
To cover the cracks.

Delivered the babies
When lambing time came,
Guided small hands
To write their own name.

Whipped up a meal
For thrashers, from scratch,
Planted and picked
And canned from the patch.

Plucked from the top
Of the old cherry tree,
Fruit too elusive
For Dad, Sis or me.

The list could go on,
It's only begun
To tell all the things
That Mom's hands have done.

So I can't help smiling
When I see Mom so chic,
Then look at her hands
With nails short and thick.

I think of the love
Those hands have bestowed
While guiding five kids
Down the straight narrow road;

And I'm proud of my Mom
And her versatile ways,
And want her to know it
The rest of her days.

LAND MARKS

A lonely sentinel on a Western hill,
Is the shepherd's landmark, standing still;
A crude affair – just a pile of rock,
But an unfailing guide for shepherd and flock.

Weathered and beaten by the wind and the sand,
A silent post in a barren land.
No glittering lights, no siren sound,
Just a rough heap of stones that the shepherd found.

But the shepherd's faith in that heap has been cast,
And he trusts it's worth, thru' calm and blast.
This teaches us to never disdain
Life's simple things, tho' they are rough, crude or plain.

For many a traveler has lost his way,
Dazed by the glare and noise of the day;
But many a man, his bearings found,
Because a land-mark, crude, firmly stood it's ground.

SPUNK

Oh, I hear that you are battered,
That you're purple and you're blue -
But you haven't lost your gumption,
That you're still the same old you!

Now the world has tried to get you down,
Many times before -
And they've said you were a goner -
Had you right down on the floor;
But you always got up swingin'
Before the count of ten,
And we know that Mathis spunk
Will do it once again!

So even tho' you're down again,
And your right arm is bereft,
Just stand up on those wobbly legs,
And let 'em have it with a left!

(Written for 'Mom' Mathis, who at the age
of 65, lost her right arm in an auto acci-
dent, but within a year was back at her
painting and sewing.)

INTESTINAL FORTITUDE

Oh, they've pricked him and they've poked him,
Cut him open, sewed him shut –
And they've rearranged his entrails,
But he still has lots of guts.

He has lost his brawny muscles
And he's scarred from all the cuts,
But he never lost his grit,
And he still has lots of guts.

He's been weak just like a baby,
And felt foolish as a nut.
Yes, they've messed up all his innards,
But he still has lots of guts.

Oh, we healthy ones may grumble
And wallow in our ruts,
But here's a guy who won't give up –
He's still got lots of guts!

GRAMMA'S PURPLE COAT

A child-hood wish had our dear Mother –
We'd sometimes hear her quote,
"If I someday could have my 'druthers',
I'd like a purple coat."

The years went by, kids left the nest,
Gram's wish was never granted;
(Tho' she had always done her best
To keep us dressed and panted!)

Then came the year when Gram turned eighty
And Christmas time drew close.
We kids tho't Grampa and his lady
Should have some nicer clothes.

We went to town, against their will,
And pushed thru' crowded streets.
Gramp scorned the noisy, rushing mill,
And sought a place to rest Gram's feet.

No coat in town took Gramma's eye,
And many didn't fit;
Until, in one last, weary try,
Her eyes with joy a-lit.

A purple coat? – 'Twas not our choice,
But Gram was satisfied.
It made her aged heart rejoice,
And she took it home with pride.

Gram wore her purple coat,
As tickled as a kid;
And tho' she said we shouldn't dote,
We're mighty glad we did;

For after Christmas, Gramma died
And now is laid to rest.
But a child-hood wish was gratified,
And in knowing that, we're blessed.

GRAMPA AT THE CIRCUS

Who's first to say, "Let's go!",
When circus day comes on?
Who's first into the car,
And anxious to be gone?   GRAMPA

Who choses ring-side seats
So nothing will be missed?
Who buys the first balloon
And ties it to my wrist?   GRAMPA

Who gets so dry and thirsty
Underneath the old Big Top?
Who signals for the boy
And buys us all some pop?   GRAMPA

Who holds his breath in awe
As acrobats whirl 'round?
Who snickers like a kid
At antics of the clown?   GRAMPA

Who's hungry for a 'dog,
And then some salty corn?
Who's got to have more pop,
As sure as he is born?   GRAMPA

(Cont'd)

Who's wispy graying hair
Is blowing in the breeze?
Who cranes his neck to watch
The swinging high trapeeze?   GRAMPA

Who's having most the fun,
A-judging by his grin?
Fluffs of cotton candy
A-clinging to his chin.   GRAMPA

Who tells it all at home
To those with listn'ing ear?
Who's twinkling eyes betray
He's relived a by-gone year?   GRAMPA

Who's tired and full at nite,
His supper he can't eat?
Who falls asleep, content,
This day has been complete?   GRAMPA

OLD-TIME COW-BOY

The rocking-chair is empty –
The red one by the door,
And Cliff, the old-time cow-boy
Will sit in it no more.

How often were the times
We stopped in for a chat,
And there was Cliff to greet us
In his battered old felt hat.

A hankerchief about his neck –
His cane there in his hand,
And we'd ask to hear again,
His cow-boy tales so grand.

We'd listen, eager-eyed,
As he spoke with Western charm,
One bowed and weary leg
Draped across the rocker's arm.

He'd tell of days gone by
When he was but a child,
How he joined the hardy band
To tame the West so wild.

He told of danger on the plains,
Of ranch and homestead life,
And how the trail was often eased
By a faithful horse and wife.

But Cliff took sick one snowy morn
As in his chair he sat,
And on the way to Doctor's help,
He died, wearing his old hat.

We'll miss this old-time cow-boy,
A link with days of yore;
But we'll see him in our mem'ry
In his rocker by the door.

COW-BOY'S HUMILIATION
or
CONFOUND FRACTURE

"Danger is my business",
I'd oft' been heard to brag,
As I'd don my spurs and chaps
And saddle up my nag.

I'd often tho't it noble -
If I should e'er be thrown
From off a buckin' bronco,
And break near ev'ry bone.

I'd never whine at torture
Or scars upon my hide
When I'd conquered bull or bronc
And made 'em let me ride.

I'd join my cow-boy buddies
For coffee after ten
And we'd each show off our wounds
And tell it all again.

They would slap me on the back,
"Why, who'd'a ever thunk
Such a spindly-legged kid
Would demonstrate such spunk!"

I'd say, "Aw, it was nothin' ",
And they would ask for more
And I'd tell another tall one
About the scars I bore.

But here I am, all boogered up,
Right arm in a sling -
Can't hardly get my chaps on
Or do a single thing.

(Cont'd.)

And when they ask what happened,
I hang my head in shame,
'Cause how I got this break
Would disgrace a cow-boy's name.

For I was bein' foolish –
Forsook a cow-boy rule
And turned my back on horse-flesh
And harnessed up a mule!

I wish I'd never done it –
Why wasn't I more smart?
That crazy mule took off
And I toppled out the cart.

Could anything more lowly,
Could anything more crude
Happen to a cow-boy?
You'd think I was a dude!

You who'd be my friend –
If you really want to be it –
Don't gawk at my right arm –
Pretend that you don't see it!

I've got problems all enough –
Humiliation's cruel –
And I feel like goin out
And standin' 'hind that mule!

MALE AND FEMALE MADE HE THEM

No man his body ever hated
Paul the Apostle has related.
And truer words were never uttered,
For at his flesh, man's never sputtered.
What man would stand before his mirror
And curse his waist-line or posterior?
What male would primp more hours than lawful,
Then wail to all, "Don't I look awful?"?
A man delights in his own body,
Tho' it's wrinkled and fat and poddy.
If one lonesome hair's upon his chest,
Man will brag that his hair is the best!
No, man his body will not despise
His flesh and bones are his joy and prize.

But a woman's from a diff'rent ilk.
Tho' she's dressed in satin or in silk
She'll wish her hair was a diff'rent hue,
That her eyes were brown instead of blue,
Her waist-line smaller, bust-line bigger,
Why must she have such awful figger?
She hates her freckles, her up-turned nose;
Her feet are ugly - so are her toes.
She's in her bood-wah, combing, painting,
And now emerges, still complaining,
"Oh, I really look just like a sight -
My hair won't do any-thing tonight!"
Husband, boy-friend, father - hear, ye!
You'd best play it safe and don't agree!

SPRING FORGIVENESS

Broad Wyoming has its' woes –
Dusty, gusty wind that blows.
Fills our eyes and teeth with grit –
Cannot see and cannot spit.
Wind that tries to wear us down,
Blows our crops right out the ground;
Mocks us, shocks us in disgust;
Still it howls and brings its' dust.

Weary women, clean in vain.
Calves, keep bawling on the plain.
Ranchers, Farmers, curse and fret –
Wyoming's wind is blowing yet.

But, Wyoming, we'll forgive,
If you'll only let us live
Thru' the winter, into spring
When meadow-larks begin to sing.
Hushed will be our unkind words
When we hear those lovely birds
Singing gayly in their nests,
Reminding us that West is best.

When at last you're penitent,
For a time, your strength is spent,
Wind, be pleased to give us rest,
Bringing spring-time to the West.

Gladly will we cease to wail,
Forget the dust, forgive the hail,
Look beyond this tree-less plain,
Remember not the lack of rain,
If only once we're blessed to hear
That song of hope, that voice of cheer.
Wyoming, we'll excuse your wrongs
When meadow-larks begin their songs.

Then when the wind resumes its chant
(And stop it, we most surely can't!) –
We'll remember brighter days,
When meadow-larks burst forth in praise.

A TRIBUTE TO THE OLD TIMERS

"Old Timers" - we call 'em, that sturdy band
Who left home and friends to come to this land.
From Kansas, Missouri and Iowa state,
Eager, they came, not knowing their fate.
From Texas, Nebraska and way back East,
Came parents and children, belongings and beast;
Setting their faces t'ward new frontiers,
Braving the wilds, the storms and the fears.
Not heeding the warnings, dreadful and black,
Of friend and foe, who were sure they'd be back.
Seeking a place to call their own,
Leaving behind the familiar, well known.

"Old Timers" - we call 'em, that motley crew
Who left the old in search of the new.
There were Russians, and Germans, Danes and Swedes,
A mixture of bloods, of backgrounds and creeds.
Onward they came, by ox, horse or stage,
By wagon, by train, the youth and the aged.
Bringing new life with seeds and a plow,
With little, with much, a calf or a cow.
A doctor, a farmer, a teacher, a cook -
A rancher, a merchant and sometimes a crook.
Joining the coyotes, the bob-cats, the snakes,
An assortment of folks who had what it takes.

"Old Timers" - these folks who braved the forces,
(Hard was the lot for women and horses.)
Who birthed their babies in their own small home;
Never sure those babies would be full grown.
For disease and snakes and guns were cruel
And death in a home was often the rule.
The graves on the hill in silence relate
Stories of losses of children or mate.
Tragedies, illnesses, sudden or slow
All took their toll in those days long ago.
Life in the West was not easy back then,
But brave and staunch were its' women and men.

(cont'd.)

"Old Timers" - those folks who knew what it meant
To go without needs, to be weary and spent,
To battle the hail, the wind and the dust,
Ready to quit in despair and disgust -
To start once again, hitch up the britches,
Assured life was meant for more than riches;
To share the feeling of brother-hood,
When times were bad or times were good;
To know you'd a neighbor, more than ready,
Who'd stay in a crises, calm and steady,
Who'd open his home to stranger or friend,
As free to borrow as he was to lend.

"Old Timers" - folks with lingo all their own
(To those who came West were its' secrets known) -
They speak of sour dough, Injuns and cavvy -
Words that an Easterner couldn't savvy;
Cow chips and wind-lass, shanties and soddies;
Trail drivers, homesteads, long horns and waddies;
Blow outs and hail outs, plus forts and cow-pokes,
Spoken by suntanned and bow-legged folks,
Who cut their teeth on biscuits and jerkey,
Adding sometimes a deer or a turkey -
Nicknamed Andy, or Jake, Shotts, Bump or Cliff -
Down-to-earth folks, never stuck up or stiff.

"Old Timers" - those people who took delight
In a gay song fest on a starry night
(Fun and pleasure was not costly back then,
Like camping out on the way to Cheyenne.)
They rejoiced when at last the mail came thru'
Six days of the week instead of just two,
And thrilled at the sound of the first black train,
Whistling and puffing thru' the hills and plain.
They knew what it was with no church nor school,
No teacher nor Pastor with golden rule.
So, pooling their funds, they all worked as one,
'Til both church and school were at last begun.
                              (Cont'd.)

"Old Timers" – hardy men with loyal wives,
Who came to the West to carve out their lives.
Many have gone now, but mem'ries are bright
Of those old timers who fought a good fight;
And left a legacy for us to claim,
Not in silver or gold or earthly fame;
But valor and courage are ours to share –
May we claim them now as a grateful heir;
Nor treat them with scorn as a useless thing,
But leave them instead to our own off-spring.
Then we will be honored in their young eyes,
If, like these Old Timers, we're prudent, wise.

FOUR IN THE FIRE

There were four in the fire - not three alone
When the Hebrew lads in the fire were thrown -
Those boys who refused to idols to turn,
And were cast in the cruel furnace to burn.

Four in the fire - and the fourth was no less
Than the Son of God - Who was there to bless
And protect His brethren from smoke and flame,
And bring them all forth to extol His name.

Yes, four in the fire, and when they returned
They smelled not of smoke, neither were they burned.
And all that they lost in that firey blast,
Were the fetters that bound and held them fast.

Another's in the flame, God's child, with you
When the firey trials you're called to go thru'.
He'll stay thru' the heat, and then lead you out
With no hurt, no bonds, the vic'try to shout.

CHRIST IN YOU - THE HOPE OF GLORY

BOLD EXPERIMENT.. God's treasure in a vessel of clay!
Doth He not fear to exhibit His glory this way?

Will not we, faltering and failing, misuse this treasure
Freely bestowed, running over, full measure?

Should not He safe-guard this Pearl of great price?
Eternal Spirit in an earthen pot - is He wise?

Oh, the depths of His wisdom, surpassing my sight so dim -
His treasure's in earthen vessels, that the glory may go
                    to Him!

THE DEPARTURE

I stood last night at Heaven's door
And watched my loved one enter in.
No holding back -
No fear to take the final step,
But eager to begin
The endless joys awaiting him.

Oft to that door, He'd come before -
Exhausted, spent, and wracked with pain;
But closed it had remained -
Until last night,
He caught the gleam of Heaven's light
And knew it ope'd for him.

Farewells he gave to one and all,
Then left us with a song,
And bade us meet him on that shore
To join with him the throng,
And sing thru' out the endless years
The praise of Him Who ope's the door
And wipes away our tears.

FROM FOOT-STOOL TO THRONE

They sat on the rough wooden benches under the big revival tent. A bright-eyed girl of about seven and two tousle-headed boys, probably five and nine, squeezed between the young parents. A gurgling baby was perched on Daddy's knee.

Those of us who knew this family were surprised to see them there. The father hadn't been out of the hospital very long. His face and eyes showed it. Lately his hospital visits had become more frequent, as Hodgkin's disease slowly sapped away his life.

Raising my voice with the hundreds of others, I suddenly choked on the words of "When We All Get to Heaven." That family behind me - with the shadow of death hovering over them - were singing at the top of their voices, "just one glimpse of Him in glory, will the toils of life repay." Then the song leader led us in "When the Roll is Called Up Yonder, I'll Be There." Again I was overwhelmed with emotion as I heard those childish voices joining their parents in victorious song. They sang without tremor or hesitation, voicing each word with meaning and assurance.

I felt insincere and shallow, thinking of how often I'd glibly sung those words. This family sang from their hearts, knowing that heaven was not a vague, far-off place. Its doors might open any day for Daddy.

There were other services, in between hospitalizations, when we saw them - always together and always radiant.

Some months later, heaven's doors did open. Sensing his moments were limited, the father called together the adult members of his family, brother, sisters, parents. Slowly, with effort, he bade each one farewell, expressing his love and concern for the ones who knew not his Saviour. Then he asked for scripture reading and a song. As the closing, trembling words of "What a Friend We Have in Jesus" filled that hallowed room, the young father slipped away.

Today that brave mother and children sing without the reassurance of Daddy's voice. But they look forward to the roll call, when all together in heaven, they will join him in triumphant song.

As for me, I sing more thoughtfully these days.